ADULT COLORING BOOK
Female Warriors

This book belongs to

_____

_____

Copyright@2021 BLONDEA
All rights reserved

The scanning, uploading, and distribution of this book without author permission is a theft of the author intellectual property.

The purchaser of this book may scan or copy for personal use only. You may post colored page on social media if complemented by an artist credit and the title of the book.

If you have any question or concerns let us know at support@blondea.com

Thank you for your support of the author's right.

Damita Victoria is a Coloring Book brand owned by BLONDEA. BLONDEA is a company based in France.

Published by BLONDEA
www.blondea.com

COLORING TIPS

We have printed the art in single-sided pages. Each image is placed on its own black-backed page to reduce the bleed-through to the next image. If you are using markers, it strongly recommended sliding a piece of cardstock or the thick paper behind the page you are working on to make sure the ink doesn't stain the next page.

We provided double images placed in version 1 and version 2. Therefore, you will be able to color your favourite art twice incase you want to have a different version of each artwork. You can also keep an extra copy in case you make a coloring mistake.

Now Relax and enjoy the "ME" Time :)

COLORING TIPS

✏ - This icon will show you where to fill in with your coloring pencil/marker/brush

The grey areas indicate exactly where in the face the sense of depth becomes greater so we have a better understanding of dimension.

Usually the shadow can be noticable if the light is frontal and it has a low intensity. It also tends to show more in the space between the eye and the eyebrow, on the nose bridge and the nose tip, under the cheeks and on the neck.

Go ahead and fill in all the white and grey shadow areas where the skin is supposed to be with a color that resembles that of the human flesh.

To achieve that look it is adviced to use a light brown color and remember to be careful with the pressure you put on the paper with the coloring pen's tip, or the number of brush strokes because that directly impacts how light or dark the skin tone is going to be.

For a lighter skin tone, use the pen tip very softly, and for a darker skin tone push the tip of the pen a bit harder or go over the first layer of color a few times. If you want to go for a more fantasy inspired look like a blue, green or purple skin, go ahead and use the same logic of pen pressure mentioned up above.

Use the same method to fill in with color the areas where tattoos or faces paint designs are supposed to be. Make sure to use a darker toned color compared to the color you previously used for the base layer of the skin.

COLORING TIPS

Next, if you want to add more depth to the drawing and make it look more realistic, proceed to add some colour in the same areas the grey shadow was in the first step.

Make sure to use a darker tone than the base colour you used for the skin. You can use colours such as dark brown or red depending on the skin base color you have used initially.

You can also use black as well but only for the eyes to give a mysterious ombre look.
Do not use black for the nose, cheeks or neck area!

In case you want to add some life or warmth to the face you can try adding a light touch of red or rosey pink colour to the nose, cheeks and chin. Please make sure to be careful and use only light strokes of colour and not overdo it otherwise you won't achieve the look you were going for!

As a side tip, in case you want to add freckles or other skin texture such as beauty marks , apply hard tiny strokes of a dark brown-ish color.

The last step which is "Highlights" might be considered a bit more challenging compared to the other steps and you have to be very careful when applying it.
For this step you might want to use a white gel pen and a white chalk pencil.

With the white gel pen you should apply the sharpest points/dots of light which are usually located on the areas inside the eye, the tip of the nose, lips and middle of the chin.

On the other hand the white chalk pencil gives a more soft shiny look and the areas where you might want to apply that are the corners of the eye(tear duct area), the side of the cheek to add dimension, under the cheek area for a better contouring, the forehead and the side of the neck.

If you do not own neither of the objects mentioned above then you can try achieving a similar highlight effect by darkening the other part of the face that should not be highlighted.

COLORING TIPS

Highlighted Areas will indicate the area where the flow on the lips will show more.

When the highlighted area has the same colour tone as the lips it is called a matte finish look.

If the highlights have a strong white colours to them then the look can be considered as highly glossy.

If the highlights are just slightly lighter than the base lip colour, it is considered a satin finish lipstick.

To add a touch of realism, try adding dark shadows with a colour that is a tone darker than the base lip colour used.

As a final touch, to make the look even more realistic, try adding some outer highlight under the upper and bottom lip with a white chalk pencil.

PART 1

PART 2

DISCOVER OUR OTHER BOOKS THAT YOU'LL LOVE!

New-Fashioned Princesses	☐	Pin-Up Models	☐
Adult Mandala Coloring Pages	☐	Happy Season	☐
Beautiful Women	☐	Calm and Cozy	☐
100 AMAZING Mandala	☐	Christmas Mandalas	☐
Fantastic Beauties Book One	☐	Winter Aesthetic	☐
Fantastic Beauties Two	☐	Lovely Garden	☐
Classy Princesa	☐	Whimsical Dreams	☐
Relaxing Scenery	☐	Flourish Swirls	☐
Chill Out in Paris	☐	Editorial Fashion	☐
Intricate Patterns	☐	Positive Affirmations Book One	☐
Summer on the Farm	☐	Positive Affirmations Book Two	☐
Magical Wildland	☐	Victorian Fashion	☐
By The Beach	☐	Love is Everwhere	☐
Fantasticaland	☐	Decorative Patterns	☐
Flowery Beauties	☐	Zen Scenery	☐
Happy Summer!	☐	100 Easy Flowers	☐
Charmer Beauty	☐	Fantasialand	☐
Freaky Night	☐	Floating Life	☐
Relaxing Winter	☐	Magical Fairies	☐
Animal Reading Books	☐	Floral Mandalas	☐
The Witches	☐	Female Warriors	☐
100 Coloring	☐	Cozy Interiors	☐
Hello Autumn!	☐		
Mandala Flowers	☐		
Fantastic Beauties Book Three	☐		
Beautiful Patterns	☐		
Relaxing Mandalas	☐		
100 Easy Mandalas	☐		

GET FREE COLORING PAGE

We publish a free coloring page regularly in our Facebook group. Join now, and let's have fun together!

FACEBOOK GROUP: DAMITA VICTORIA ARTWORK

LET'S BE FRIENDS

Damita Victoria

www.damitavictoria.com

WRITE AMAZON REVIEWS

WE'D LOVE YOUR FEEDBACK...

We'd love to know how everything worked out for you, don't be a stranger! Join the conversation and share your feedback with us.

Find this book on Amazon, scroll to the customer reviews, and please let us know your thoughts and comments.

We'd love to hear your feedback so we can continue to improve our service to you.

Printed in Great Britain
by Amazon